Drinking Alone by Moonlight

(An anthology of Chinese verse)

To Theo, with very best wishes for 2022 from Ian and Jade

Ian Watts and Jade Wei Watts

3P PUBLISHING

Text Copyright © Ian Watts 2021

Ian Watts has asserted their right in accordance with the Copyright Designs and Patents Act 1988 to be identified as the author of this work.

All rights reserved.

No part of this publication may be lent, resold, hired out or reproduced in any form or by any means without prior written permission from the authors and publisher.

All rights reserved.

Copyright © 3P Publishing

First published in 2021 in the UK.

3P Publishing

C E C, London Road Corby

NN17 5EU

ISBN: 978-1-913740-37-5

Cover Design: James Mossop

*Dedicated, with love, to our three daughters
Cassandra, Rhiannon and Hui Ying*

Foreword

I know nothing about Chinese poetry. Or at least, I used to know nothing about Chinese poetry. That was until 2015 when Ian Watts began coming to our poetry night, Run Your Tongue, and started sharing his translations with us. It was here where Ian met sponsor, speaker and publisher Andy Gibney, and the rest – as they say – is history. Ian became a regular and favourite at our nights in Kettering, bringing with him a seemingly endless supply of translations of Chinese poetry. I remember thinking at the time that one of the most striking things about them was that (if we ignore momentarily any historical and cultural references) it felt as though they could have been written a few weeks ago rather than a fair few centuries ago (in reality, the translations had been written a few weeks ago, but you know what I mean). Not only does this highlight the fact that many of the poems deal with themes still relevant today – loss and longing, conflict and suffering – but it also reveals the skill of the translator by enabling these poems to connect with a modern audience. When the pandemic hit in March 2020, Run Your Tongue moved online, and Ian continued to share – live from Kettering – while our audience broadened across the world to Australia, Morocco and North America.

The pandemic also meant that Ian was separated from his wife, Jade, who was still in China for the duration of the lockdowns and cancelled international travel. Or rather, Ian was stuck in Kettering and wasn't able to join her. Either way, there was an enforced focus on the collection, and Jade collaborated with Ian on the translations even though they were thousands of miles apart. Whilst most of us were taking up gardening, cooking or attempting to complete Netflix, Ian and Jade worked tirelessly on translating these wonderful traditional Chinese poems into English.

It would be a cliché to call this book a labour of love, but that is exactly what it is. For Ian, this journey started many years ago as a TEFL teacher in Kettering and then, whilst teaching English as a Foreign Language in (what was then) Czechoslovakia, he began writing translations of Czech poems into English (I've been told that, like Chinese, Czech is another notoriously difficult language to master). Years later, his teaching would take him to China, where he met Jade. In 2015, he published Careful Drowning – predominantly because he was disappointed by the available English translations of popular Chinese poetry – and the poems that appeared in that collection find themselves here along with many, many others.

As an English Literature tutor, spoken word night host and Creative Writing PhD student, poetry and words touch pretty much every aspect of my life. However, it wasn't always that way. For the whole five years of my secondary education, my English teacher was intent on sucking the life out of the subject. It wasn't until I had finished school and began to discover poetry that wasn't taught in the narrow scope of the English Literature syllabus that I could really connect and eventually fall in love with it. One of my favourite things about poetry at the time (and even now) was that I could open a book and have an instant connection with a person I've never met or likely to meet (usually because they were long since dead or because they were highly unlikely to visit Kettering). The poet shares that moment with you for about the length of a page and sends a message through the ages. When reading these new translations, I'm taken to a place thousands of miles away and hundreds of years ago, sharing that moment, that experience with the writer and sometimes even drinking alone by moonlight with them.

This collection contains many of the most popular poems written in Chinese and has 3000 years of recorded Chinese poetry from which to choose. In the Tang era alone, which spanned from the 7th to the 10th Century CE, over 50,000 poems survive. So, whilst translating these 100 or so poems was surely something of a herculean effort, they can only offer a brief glance into the wealth of Chinese poetry available. Ian makes short notes at the end of some of the poems, but I believe that they stand alone without any background information. However, some of the stories behind the poems are just as fascinating as the works themselves.

War and conflict feature throughout the collection – not always as main themes – but we know they are always lurking somewhere, ominously in the background. In 'Poem Finished in Seven Steps' by Cao Zhi and dating from the 5th Century CE, the poet's brother, Cao Pi, suspected Cao Zhi of treason and decided to have him executed. He told Cao Zhi to take seven steps and, on pain of death, compose a poem in that time. Cao Zhi completed his task and survived.

In the 10th Century CE, Li Yu was overthrown as the Emperor of Southern Tang. After two years as a prisoner, he was 'offered' the chance to take poison rather than spending the rest of his life in prison. Emperors were believed to be related to the gods, and so perhaps no one fancied becoming the gods' enemy by killing him. He wrote 'The Beauty of Yu' just before he died.

You will also notice that distance and separation is a recurring theme throughout the collection, perhaps appropriate for our current times and how this book was written. These poems were originally written long before the modern technology that we seem so inseparable from today. We can be instantly connected to someone on the other side of the globe at the touch of a button; in this collection, we often meet speakers compelled to travel across the vast, ancient country for many reasons.

You will also meet poets who express their disgust with many aspects of society, including in the anonymous 'Rat in the Field', which rails against corrupt local officials. The incredibly sad 'The Old Serving Maid in the Palace' by Bai Juyi expresses sorrow at the many young women chosen to be concubines.

With these new translations, Ian will undoubtedly

allow readers to enter a world unknown to them. Others will revisit a familiar world in a new light through beautiful imagery blended with moments of humour and moments of extreme sadness.

Rob Reeves
July 2021

Contents

Introduction	1
Drinking Alone by Moonlight	4
The Osprey's Call	5
Rat in the Field	7
Ode to an Orange Tree	9
Seeing off Du Shaofu to be a Governor in Shuzhou	12
Southern Yangtze	13
Going Back to my Hometown	15
Chant for Willows	15
Liangzhou Song	16
Spending the Night on the Jian De River	17
Bells Ringing in the Rain	18
Spring Dawn	21
Missing Xin on a Summer's Day in the South	22
Marching	24
Seeing off Xin Jian at Fu Rong Tower	25
From the Stork Tower	26
3,5,7 Words	27
Song of Leaving the Pass	29
Seeing off Yuan Er on the Road to An Xi	30
Leaving White Emperor City	31
Dreaming I Roamed on Tian Mu Mountain	32
Visiting Xian Mountain to See the Taoist Who Priest Wasn't There	36

The Changgan Song	37
The Hard Road to Shu	40
Invitation to Drink	45
War to the South of the City	49
Three Pure and Peaceful Songs	51
Thoughts on a Quiet Night	55
Endlessly Yearning to be in Changgan	56
Hard Walking on the Road	57
Joking with Du Fu	59
Waking up Drunk on a Spring Day, Talking about Aspirations	60
Marble Steps Complaint	62
Saying Goodbye to Librarian Shu Run at Xie Tiao Tower	63
Sitting Alone on Jingting Mountain	64
The Farewell Pavilion	65
Gazing at the Waterfall at Lu Mountain, Far Away	65
To Meng Haoran	67
To Wang Lun	68
Remembering Qin E	69
Seeing Off Meng Haoran at the Yellow Crane Tower	71
Sweet Rain on a Spring Night	72
Soldiers and Carts on the Road to War	73
Docking Near Feng Jiao Bridge at Night	75
Strolling by the River, Alone, Looking at the Flowers	76
Feeling Sorry for the Farmer	78
Poem Finished in Seven Steps	79

Song of the Departing Son	79
A Lyre	80
Autumn Moon	81
Remembering Events at Red Cliff (to the tune of 'Charming Nian Nu')	83
On the New City Road	86
Impromptu Poem	88
A Joke for Zhang Xian	88
To His Dead Wife	90
Written on the Wall of Xilin	92
Monastery Poem to Li Bai	93
An Invitation to Liu Shijiu	94
To the Tune of 'The Beauty of Yu'	95
Buying Peonies (to the tune of 'Buddhist Dancers')	97
Harem Poem	98
Arrogant Eunuchs	99
The Old Serving Maid in the Palace	101
Drinking and Looking at the Peonies	104
Homecoming after Work	105
The Complaint in Spring	106
Bird Cries from the Ravine	107
Jottings	108
The Goose Chant	109
Sent North on a Rainy Night	110
To the Tune of 'Slow Tunes'	110

Tipsy	112
Plums Fall Down	113
Looking at the Moon and Missing Those I Care About Who are Far Away	115
Listening to the Zither	116
Crossing the Han River	117
Drinking Wine	118
In Memoriam	119
Delayed Return from Shu	120
To the Tune of 'Song of a Bamboo Branch'	121
Rural Scene By the River Wei	122
Upset in the West Palace in Autumn	123
Your Behaviour in Your Youth	124
The Cock is Crowing From the Shi Jing	124
Seeing West Lake from the Wanghu Pavilion	126
Drove my Carriage	128
Missing my Shandong Brothers at Double Ninth Festival	129
To Li Dan and Yuan Xi	130
Yearning for Home	131
Song of Chi Sai	132
The Blossoming Tree	134
Poets and their Dates	135

Introduction

At the top is heaven where the gods live in their jade palace. Below that is the sky where the paths of the sun and moon chariots can be traced. Below that is the earth, where men and women live and die, except for the emperor. He is a direct descendant of the gods, so, when he dies, he joins the gods. Traditionally, Chinese people are buried on hillsides; the higher up the hill, the better, because it is closer to heaven. Feng shui says so. Dead souls go to Diyu where there are 18 levels for them to atone for their sins. This is the belief structure of the universe in which, by and large, Chinese poets operated.

Chinese people still celebrate their dead at the Qing Ming (tomb cleaning) festival. Some people still worship their ancestors and carry out their Confucian filial duties of praying to the ancestors and burning joss money for the dead to spend. Nowadays, others just go through the motions. Sometimes, they set off massive firecrackers so that the dead can't hear them crying. Incidentally, it is very bad luck to leave a cemetery with the ash from burnt, fake money on your person because a spirit may follow you to get his money back and bring you bad luck.

For an atheist country, the Chinese can be very superstitious.

All of this is reflected in their literature through the ages. Poetry has been a central part of Chinese life for almost 3,000 years.

The oral tradition was the basis for the development of written poetry. In fact, the ability to write a poem was part of the Confucian exam system for joining the elite civil service. The people who were literate for many centuries were a tiny fraction of the populace. The authors of the poems, herein, range from emperors to peasants.

This book is not a book about Chinese poetry, it is a book of popular Chinese verse. As such, notes accompanying some poems had to answer the question: "Does this note assist the reader?" We have not assumed any knowledge of Chinese in the translations and notes. Nor have we assumed any knowledge of phonetics on the part of readers. We have included approximations of sounds to assist those who wish to read translations aloud, chu pronounced choo, for example. Wherever there is a place name, we have tried to supply the modern location.

Events

Several events, mainly occurring during the last 100 years, have influenced the growth of interest in Chinese poetry. The People's Republic of China was formed in 1949. It made Mandarin the official language of China. It adopted pinyin as the official system of romanisation of the Chinese language. It introduced simplified Chinese. It is sad that many translators and their lazy publishers still refer to the old Wade Giles system of expressing Chinese in

English. Mao Zedong's name is not Mao Tse Tung, nor has it ever been. In 2019, nationally, every Chinese school student has to be able to recite some poems. Some teachers amongst us might say it is better to truly understand a smaller number of poems. Luckily, for the students and teachers alike, many Chinese poems are short, Li Bai's 'Thoughts on a Quiet Night' is only four lines long, for example.

During the Cold War, many Americans believed that learning Chinese was unpatriotic. Since then, and following the demise of the Cultural Revolution, China has gradually opened up to the West. Every Chinese child learns some English now. Much more Chinese literature is now available to the rest of the world and vice versa.

This collection is a collection of popular poems translated into English. It does not claim to be representative of all Chinese poetry; that would be a much larger collection. It contains, unintentionally, most of the poems that end up in some people's lists of top Chinese poems. There is no way that a translated work can compare with the original. It is impossible, in our view, to match the original verse form, and we haven't tried to. Have a look at Li Bai's 3, 5, 7 poem. Here, there are three translations, 3,5,7, syllables, 3,5,7, words and a free translation. Which is your favourite?

Our guiding light has been to try and convey the meaning and feeling of the original.

All mistakes are ours alone, as are all the photos.

Drinking Alone by Moonlight
by Li Bai

Drinking alone from a jug of wine,
No friends are here with me,
I raise a toast to the shining moon,
Under the blossoming tree,
For, we together make three.
Moonlight, my shadow, and me.

But the moon doesn't drink,
And my shadow slinks,
Dolefully, at my side,
Yet, my shadow's my servant,
And the moon is my friend,
And I will make merry,
Before the Spring's end!
Moonbeams follow the songs I chant,
And my shadow follows my weaving dance,
Sober, the three of us shared the fun,
Drunk, our separate courses run.
We'll meet again in Eternity,
Moonlight, my shadow, and me.

The Osprey's Call
by Anonymous

From the island in the river,
An osprey keeps on calling,
The dream girl I'd like to catch is
Graceful and enthralling.
River plants grow in patches,
You can pick them on either side

The dream girl I can't quite catch is
The one I always miss,
In waking or in sleeping,
My thoughts are ever this,
River plants grow in patches,
Picked left or right, it just depends,
My dulcimer will tell the lady,
That I want to be her friend.
River plants grow in patches,
Easy or hard to pick sometimes,
My lady shall hear, to make her happy,
The beating of drums and the bells sweet chimes.

☀

Notes

The first anthology of Chinese poetry, the Shi Jing, began production in the first millennium BCE 250 CE. Many of the poems are from the oral tradition, folk songs, recitations and workers' and children's chants. Most of the earliest recorded poems are anonymous.

Rat in the Field
by Anonymous

Rat in the field! Rat in the field!
Don't eat my millet! Don't eat my meal!
I've worked for you for many years.
I swear I'll go away from here
You've never cared about me,
To a happier land, a happier land,
A happier land, that is my plan

Rat in the field! Rat in the field!
Don't eat my wheat! Don't eat my meal!
I've worked for you for many years,
I swear I'll go away from here,
From you, never a fair reward
For my hard work and all my chores,
To a happier country I will go,
A happier country where I know
I'll get to keep what's mine
Rat in the field! Rat in the field!
I swear I'll go away from here

I've worked for you for many years
From you, never a word of praise,
Don't eat young plants that I have raised
To a happier countryside I'll go
A happier countryside, with happier ways,
And who will tell of these bad days?

Ode to an Orange Tree
by Qu Yuan

Born between heaven and earth,
Local soil and water suited you,
Your command was never to move,
Living only in the South, in Chu.

You followed your only desire,
With white blossoms and dark green leaves,
With flourishing growth to make us happy,
Your ambition has been achieved.

Thorns decorate all your branches,
Your fruits are pretty and rounded,
They're painted both green and yellow,
As if by a rainbow surrounded.

Shining skin,
White within.
Like a person who has many duties,
Your growth is abundant and fine,

You're fittingly decorated,
Not ugly, but sweet and divine.

Oh yes! I know your ambition,
Is different to the rest,
Determined not to be moved,
Your courage makes you the best

Your roots go deep, you can't be moved,
Aware and independent though,
As if standing in a river,
Not going with the flow.

Your heart is unselfish and also great,
Stay calm and cautious, you'll make no mistake.

Be upstanding, fuse heaven and earth!
Let us have the same ambition,
I hope our friendship lasts for ever,
I admire your sweet condition.

Never indulgent, pretty and kind,
Your virtue a unique feature,
Strong branches and bark clearly defined,
Though young, you are my teacher.

I want to plant you in my garden,
And in my garden you will grow,
Like Bo Yi who died for his principles,
You'll be an example for me to know.

Notes

The ancient kingdom of Chu is modern day Central China, including Anhui, Hubei, Henan and Guangdong provinces.

This is a patriotic poem, and still considered as such in modern China. Transplanting the special orange tree to anywhere else had always been unsuccessful. When the harvest was ready, the fruit was picked and loaded on carts which travelled non-stop to the capital so that the emperor and his top officials could sample the fruit. Over time the tree has become a symbol of faith in one's own country, i.e. patriotism.

Seeing off Du Shaofu to be a Governor in Shuzhou
by Wang Bo

Sanqin region guards the city of Chang'an,
Watching over five ferries, in the wind and mists
Seeing you off, trying not to grieve,
We both have jobs, and you must leave,
You are my best and bosom friend,
Always, as if next door to me,
You will be far from heaven's end,
Let us not cry, as young couples do,
At this separation of me and you.

Notes

Chang'an, modern day Xi'an, was the capital city in the Tang dynasty and where the emperor dwelled, and the reference to heaven's end refers to the emperor descending from the gods. Du Shaofu was being sent to be a provincial governor. Both he and his friend were civil servants, hence the admonition in the penultimate line to keep a stiff upper lip. *Sanqin* is pronounced *San Chin*, *Chang an* is as it looks and *Suchuan* is pronounced *Soo Chwan*.

Southern Yangtze

by Anonymous

Happy harvest time for the lotus fruits!
Fishes play amongst flourishing leaves,
In the Southern reaches of the Chang Jiang river,
Fishes play, swimming hither and thither,
But then...
Fishes play to the East of the lotus leaves,
Fishes play to the West of the lotus leaves,
Fishes play to the South of the lotus leaves,
Fishes play to the North of the lotus leaves.

Notes

The Yangtze river, Chang Jiang, is up there with the giants! At Wuhan it is over 1 kilometre wide, and Wuhan is in the centre of the country. The Chinese name means Big River. The surface area of water behind the Three Gorges dam is greater than that of the UK. The river flows from Tibet to Shanghai. The poet began by writing a poem, then realised the absurdity of what he was writing, so wrote words to show how vast the river is, in all directions.

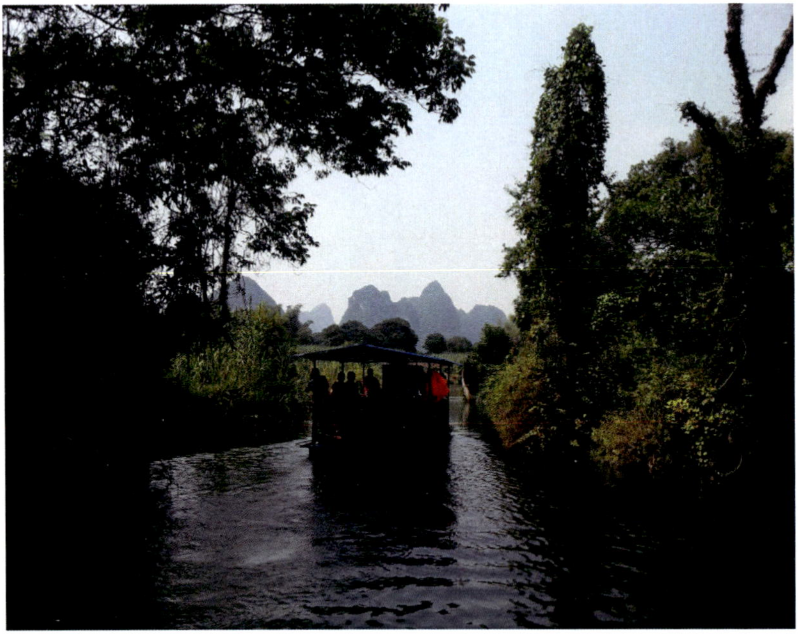

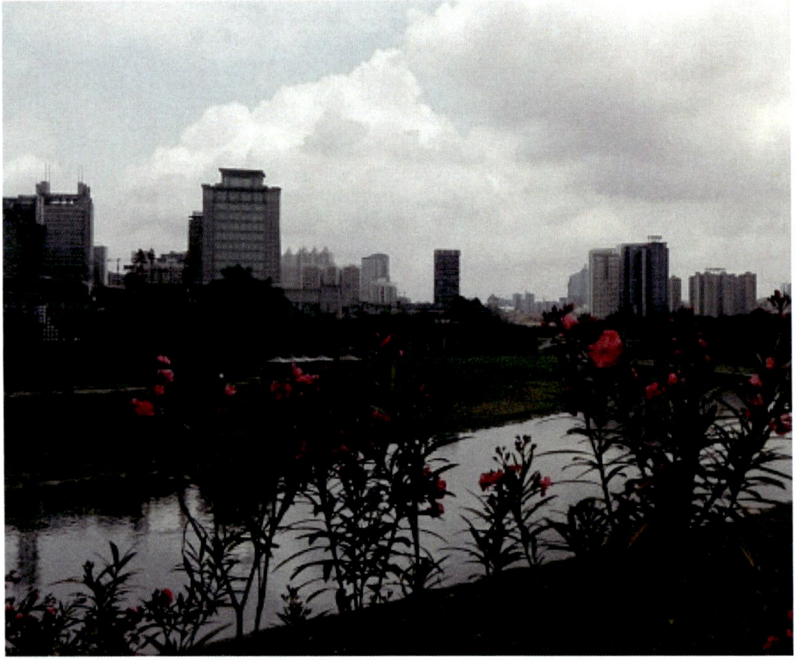

Going Back to my Hometown
by He Zhizhang

Going back to my hometown
When I was young, I left my home,
Now I'm old and have returned,
The hair round my ears has changed to white,
My accent can still be discerned,
Kids approach me, smiling, now that it's
Their chance to ask where my hometown is.

Chant for Willows

Like ribbons of silk on the trees,
Thousands of branches are bending,
All are covered with jade green leaves,
I ask who cut them all so thin?
Was it February's Spring breezes?

Liangzhou Song
by Wang Zhihuan

Waters of the Yellow River,
Fall through snow white clouds, at last,
If you want to cross the mountains,
Use the lonely Jade Gate Pass.

Don't play sad tunes upon your pipes,
Complaining that the Spring is late,
The warm Spring breezes can't be blown,
Through the lonely High Jade Gate.

Notes

The Jade Gate pass is in Gansu province, north west of Dunhuang city. It was on the silk road and strategically important for China's commerce with the West. It was also the scene, for many centuries, of China's wars with the Hun and other tribes. The sad tune he was playing was called 'The Willow Song'.

Spending the Night on the Jian De River

by Meng Haoran

With mist at dusk all around me,

At the small isle, I berth my boat,

Again, I miss my hometown,

Alone, on the river, I float,

In this wild country I see the sky,

Which is lower far than the trees,

On clear water, the moon's reflection,

Tries to get close to me.

☀

Notes

This was written about a section of the Xin An river to the west of Jian De in modern Zhejiang province.

When he stopped being a high official, Meng Haoran wanted to get back to nature, hence the idyllic feelings in the poem.

Bells Ringing in the Rain (Tune)
by Liu Yong

Cicadas sad chirping,
A late Autumn evening,
In the pavilion,
Where we are parting.

I've no desire to go out drinking,
At the tent which is next to the gate.
I hate to be leaving, they urge me to join them,
I hate to be leaving, my boat will not wait.

We two hold hands to show our emotion,
We look at each other and only have sighs,
We don't have the words to express our feelings,
This moment chokes us, tears fill our eyes.

This evening the sky is cloudy and endless,
And I must go South for one thousand li,
The saddest last moment for lovers and loved ones,

Separation and parting for my love and me.
Autumn makes the whole world dreary,
Cold and desolate the clime,
So, how can we bear our feelings,
In this sad autumnal time?

Tonight, I will be drinking heavily,
Who will know if I wake up soon?
Only the willows on the riverbank,
The cold morning wind and the sickle moon

Now we two will separate,
I've the waters to navigate.

Even if the weather is good,
Even if the scenery's fine,
It will all mean nothing to me,
Unless I hold your hand in mine.
No-one with me to share the beauty,
Nothing to give me peace of mind,
Though my heart will be full of love,
I cannot hold your hand in mine.

Notes

A li was about half a kilometre. The author was a high official, so his duty was to go where he was sent. He was expected not to be emotional at this parting.

Spring Dawn

by Meng Haoran

I slept so very well last night,

Sleeping till way past dawn,

I woke to the singing of birds,

Chatt'ring on a bright Spring morn,

Then I remembered the noise in the night,

Of wind and rain in a passing storm,

I wondered, how many blossoms

Down from the trees, might fall?

Notes

Meng Haoran had been a well respected official. He gave it all up and returned to a life of rural solitude, writing his poems.

Missing Xin Da on a Summer's Day in the South Pavilion

by Meng Haoran

The sunset comes quickly,
Behind the west mountain,
The moon rises slowly,
On the pond to the East,
And I let my hair down,
To enjoy the cool evening,
And open the window,
In this wide airy place,
I'm relaxed and content,
On the breeze is the scent,
Of sweet waterlilies,
Somewhere, dew is dripping,
From bamboo, in rhythm,
My instrument calls me,
I'll play once again,
No one to hear me play,
I miss my old friend
And so it seems,

I can only play,

For him, in my dreams.

Notes

Xin Da means Big Xin. It refers to the eldest son of the Xin (pronounced Shin) family.

Marching
by Wang Changling

Dark clouds scudding over Qinghai lake
Make snowy mountains
Appear to be black.
I look at the far Jade pass,
Far beyond our own Great Wall.
After countless battles
My armour is worn.
Unless we defeat
Enemies from the west,
I can't go home,
I know no rest.

Notes

Qinghai is pronounced *Ching high*.

Seeing off Xin Jian at Fu Rong Tower

by Wang Changling

I arrived in Wu at night,

In such terrible weather,

It seemed just like the sky

And the river had come together!

Ready for my good friend's parting,

On the following morning,

Alone, I will leave Shu mountain,

My relatives and friends,

If they ask about me, worried,

Please tell them that my heart is pure,

Like ice in jade jars, unsullied.

From the Stork Tower
by Wang Zhihuan

Yellow river flows to the sea,
Sun sets behind the mountains,
If you want to see farther,
You'll have to climb higher.

3, 5, 7 Words
by Li Bai

3,5,7 Syllables

Wind blows cold,

Moon shines bright,

Blown leaves drift, restack,

Crows fly off, fly back,

Miss you always, we can't meet,

Thinking is hard, thoughts are fleet.

3,5,7 Words

Cold Autumn wind,

Bright Autumn moon,

Windblown leaves drift, restack,

Startled crows fly off, fly back,

Missing you eternally, but we can't meet,

Tonight, my thoughts are difficult and fleet.

3, 5, 7

A sad Autumn wind is blowing,
A bright Autumn moon is showing,
Windblown leaves scatter, then restack,
Startled crows fly off, then fly back,
Lovesick and loving, missing you,
I've no idea when we shall meet,
At this moment, thinking of you,
All my thoughts disturbed and fleet.
Had I known our love's addiction,
And the pain of separation,
Right from the outset,
We should not have met.

☀

Notes

Li Bai wrote this love poem where the first couplet had three words to a line, the second couplet five words to a line and the final couplet seven words to a line. In so doing, he combined three classic verse forms. In translating this, we have produced three versions. The first is 3, 5, 7, syllables, the second 3, 5, 7, words, and the third is a free translation.

Song of Leaving the Pass
by Wang Chang Ling

It is, still, the same old moon,
And the same old practices
Are being handed down,
Through Qin and Han dynasties,
We, the soldiers, were ordered to march,
And had thousands of miles to go,
We, the soldiers, fighting the enemy,
Never returning to our homes,
The generals in Dragon city,
If they were still alive,
On Yinshan hills, they would've stopped
The Hun's relentless Southward drive.

Notes

The Hun were tribes from modern day Mongolia and beyond. The short-lived Qin dynasty unified China.

Seeing off Yuan Er on the Road to An Xi

by Wang Wei

The morning rain at Wei City

Has dampened all the dirt down,

The willows near the guest house

Look fresh and green, not brown,

I urge my departing friend

To take some wine, a parting cup,

After you cross the Yangguan Pass,

It's so hard for us to meet up.

Notes

Yuan Er means the eldest son of Yuan. Wei City is modern Xianyang in Shanxi province.

Leaving White Emperor City
by Li Bai

At dawn I leave White Emperor City,
Shrouded in colourful clouds,
From White Emperor City to Jiangling
Is about one thousand miles.
Monkeys screech from the river banks,
As my little boat takes the fast track,
I leave many mountains behind me,
It takes just one day to get back

☀

Notes

White Emperor city is modern *Chongqing*, pronounced *chongching*. Li Bai was travelling down the Yangtze river.

Dreaming I Roamed on Tian Mu Mountain
by Li Bai

Seafarers tell of fabled isles,
Veiled in mists and hard to find,
In Yue they speak of Tian Mu,
Sometimes seen, or hidden from view.

The bridge to Heaven is this mountain,
Towering over five other peaks,
Five miles high is the Tou mountain,
Just a shadow to the South East.

Over moonlit waters, on I flew,
Still dreaming of Yue and Mu,
My shadow, cast by moonlight bright,
Follows steadfastly, in the night.

I reach the site of Xie's home,
Where Shan river swiftly flows,
I hear the wild apes savage hoots,
As I put on Xie's climbing boots.

Taking me upwards through dark clouds,
Seeing sunrise over a sparkling sea,
My long slow ascent commences,
The cock of heaven crows for me.

My path ran over countless crags,
Then plunged me into darkness,
I heard, between cliffs and streams,
The growling of bears and dragons' screams.

Frightened by endless cliffs and woods,
Dark clouds threatened where I stood,
Mist rose up from swirling waters,
Roaming thunder promised slaughter,

Lightning blazed across black skies,
Smashing the mountain peaks to bits,
A cave's stone gate opened before me,
Revealing a limitless pit,
Where gold and silver palaces shone,
By the light of sun and moon,

Clothed in rainbows, dazzling bright,
The lords of the clouds came down,
Driving their chariots, riding the wind,
As phoenixes flew around.

Hither and thither,
Tigers played zithers,
As rank after rank
Of immortals passed by,
Awed to my soul
By heavenly glory,
I awoke,
With a terrified cry.
The world of mists had gone away,
Only my bedding remained, that day,
Thus, my worldly pleasures ceased,
Following waters flowing East.

Will I ever go back again?
Here's what I'd like to do,
I'll saddle a white deer,
Raised in these mountains,
And ride her back to Tian Mu…

For, how can I bow to the court

And the emperor,

When I've seen the splendour

Of all of his ancestors?

And my brow is furrowed too.

※

Notes

Li Bai was a Daoist, and Daoists believe that what you saw in a dream actually happened.

In his dream Li Bai saw the actual Immortals who were the emperor's ancestors. So, in the last verse Li Bai is hinting that the emperor does not resemble his ancestors and this puzzles him. This is the closest Li Bai can get to saying that the emperor is not immortal, and still keep his head. The fabled isles are Japan. Yue is pronounced *You eh*. Tien mu is pronounced *Tee en moo*. Xie is pronounced *She eh*, a famous mountaineer.

Visiting Daitian Mountain to See the Taoist Priest who Wasn't There

by Li Bai

Above the babbling of the brook,

Distant dogs are barking,

With dews of the morning,

Peach blossoms are sparkling,

Now and then, in the deep woods,

Deer are seen running,

At midday, no sound of noon bells ringing,

Wild bamboo pierces the dark mists of the mountain,

From the green peak springs a high soaring fountain,

No-one knows where the old priest has gone,

Sad, I lean on some pines,

As I wander alone.

The Changgan Song
by Li Bai

When my hair first covered my brow,
By the gate, I was picking flowers,
You rode up on your bamboo horse,
We played with plums, for many hours,
Together, in Changgan we lived,
Just two innocent, little kids,

At fourteen I became your bride,
Too shy to look, I turned aside,
I couldn't even smile, at all,
Or answer all your many calls.

You never lost your towering faith,
And at fifteen, I raised my head,
My only wish to stay with you,
Together until we both were dead,
No need to climb the look-out tower.

At sixteen, you went away,
Far beyond the Qutang Gorge,
Past the reef called Yanyudui.
You could not run the risk of shipwreck,
Because of all the floodings in May.

The passing of time is recorded,
By my walking outside the gate,
Where I tread is too well worn,
The sky is filled with the screech of apes.

Bit by bit, green moss is growing,
I cannot sweep the moss away,
Early autumn breezes blowing,
Leaves to the ground on a windy day.

Now in August, over the lawn,
Two yellow butterflies depart,
Over the lawn in the west garden,
Westwards, along with my sad heart.

Worry makes my young face older,

Soon you'll be returning home,

Down the river by boat from Sanba,

Send a letter, telling me so.

Then I'll try to come and greet you,

I will travel however far,

I will try my love to meet you,

And be together in Changfengsha.

Notes

Li Bai sometimes adopted a female persona to write his poems.

Navigation on the Yangtze river was a dangerous affair before the Three Gorges Dam raised the river levels considerably.

Inexplicably, Ezra Pound called this poem *The River Merchant's Wife* in what can be termed a 'loose' translation. Qutang is pronounced Chootang, Yan yu dui is pronounced Yan yoo dway.

The Hard Road to Shu
by Li Bai

Wow! So steep! So high!
More difficult to go to Shu,
Than to climb the sky!

Two emperors founded the state,
Cancong and Yufu were the last
Builders of Kingdoms in the heart of Shu,
Now, countless years have passed,

Isolated and alone,
To the west is Mount Tai Bai,
From there and on to Mount Er Mei,
Only the birds can fly.

The crest collapsed,
Five heroes were slain,
Building rope bridges
And passes again.

At the summit, the sun stopped his cart,
The sign of six dragons is there,
Far below is the loud, twisting river,
White water crashes, everywhere.

Yellow cranes won't fly over,
Apes don't dare to climb,
In crossing Mount Qingni,
The path twists and winds,
In taking one hundred steps,
You turn, at least nine times.

Your breathing is tortured,
Seeing Canjing in the sky,
And, clutching your chest,
You sit down and sigh.

I ask when will you return,
From all your travels West?
Afraid of very long journeys,
Afraid of unscaleable crests?

In ancient trees, sad birds cry,
Through dark forests,
With their mates they fly,
More difficult to go to Shu,
Than to climb the sky!

Knowing this makes beauty wither,
Mountain peaks touch each other,
Less than a foot from the sky!

Old shrivelled pines hang upside down,
Clinging to steep cliff walls,
Water smashing on the rocks,
From torrents and waterfalls.
 The sounds of rivers and streams
Echo across a thousand ravines.
This is the danger!
Tell me, oh stranger,
Why do you go there?

Mount Jiangge is high and steep,
Its valleys dangerous and deep,

One man can hold a pass,
Against an army.

Your guide may become a wolf or beast,
Killing you, for your bones, his feast.

By day, fierce tigers are menacing,
By night, giant serpents slithering,
Beasts grind their fangs before they attack,
Striking fear, drinking blood,
Like scything flax,
They slay.

From Changgan city, do not roam,
Why not go to your pleasant home?

More difficult to go to Shu,
Than to climb the sky!
Turn sideways, look West,
Then heave a sigh.

Notes

The emperor, in Changgan (Xian), facing uprisings, wanted to move his court to Shu (Sichuan). Li Bai was very much against the move. He wrote the poem to try and influence the court not to go. Cancong is pronounced *tsansong*. Canjing, pronounced *tsanjing,* is an ancient constellation.

Invitation to Drink
by Li Bai

Look!
The waters of the Yellow River
Keep falling from Heaven,
Rolling down to the sea,
Nevermore seen, by you or me!

Look now!
Look in bright mirrors in high halls!
Facing you, in the mirror,
In the morning,
Your once black hair is
white as snow,
in the evening.

Where there is a man of class,
Never let him toast the moon,
Raising an empty glass!

Since your talent is Heaven sent,
Use it! Use it! It is well spent!

A thousand silver coins to burn?
Someday, they will all return!

Pour three hundred jugs of wine,
Into one, and make it mine!
I want to get plastered,
Like any old drunkard,
Never to waken again!

A toast to master Cen,
Bring on the wine!
And to young Danqiu
Bring on the wine!

And now let me sing you a song,
Carefully listen to me,
Hear the music of drum and bell,
Eat delicious food as well,
And a life of luxury foretell!
This should not be a treasure,
By whatever measure!

We've forgotten the names
Of men who stayed sober,
Great in their times,
And forgotten again!

But oh! the best thinkers,
Were all the best drinkers,
Drunk in their time
And remembered since then!

Just like Emperor Chen who once called for,
A cask of great wine from the store.
Hand in his pocket, he pulled out ten thousand,
In order to settle the score.
They laughed as they downed it,
And when they had supped it,
They called for more wine,
And then more!

So, never say "No, the money's all gone,
And there's no more money for more"
Go and buy some good wine, and
Here's how we will settle our score,

I'll flog the old horse,
And my fur coat of course!
Tell your boy to take them away!
We'll drink to the cessation,
Of the woes of all nations,
And we will make merry, this day!

War to the South of the City
by Li Bai

This year's war on the Conghe River,
Last year's war at the Sanggan's source,
Washing weapons in Tiaozhi's seas,
Horses grazed on grasses coarse,
Growing through the snows,
On the Tian range.
Ten thousand li of battles,
Our three armies travelled,
Our troops grown weary and old,
The Xiongnu claim carnage as their own,
Ploughing the yellow sands for bones,
The only crop since ancient times.
Qin built the wall to keep them out,
Han still keep the beacons burning,
On barren lands is bloody gore,
And the wars are never ending,
Slay and be slain for evermore,
Wounded horses cry and wail,
Braying to the pitiless skies,

Vultures and hawks tear out entrails,
Then they fly off, with their prize,
To hang guts on withered branches.
On the ground are soldiers' blood stains,
As clueless generals act in vain,
Wise men know, and they have taught
That bloody war is the last resort

Notes

Conghe is pronounced *Song her.* Tiaozhi is pronounced *Tee ow zhi* (zhi as 'dg' in budge). *Tian* is pronounced *tee en.* Xiongnu is pronounced *shong noo,* known better in the West as The Hun. *Qin* is pronounced *chin.* The first Qin emperor unified China and began the Great Wall. The Han dynasty followed after the Qin.

Three Pure and Peaceful Songs
by Li Bai

Pure and Peaceful Song (number 1)

She appears robed in clouds,
With clouds all about her,
The loveliest flower they say,
And the grass where she walks,
Spreads dew all around her,
And the gentle spring breezes do play.

If you're lucky you'll see her,
At the top of Jade mountain,
Where the gods go to sport and to play,
Or else you may find her,
On Precious Jade Terrace
Where she walks at the end of the day

Pure and Peaceful Song (number 2)

On the balcony leaning,
At the Aloe pavilion,
Watching the peonies sway,
Such beauty before him
Arouses the emperor,
Who smiles and continues to gaze.

Spring breezes are warming,
And the loveliness calming,
Taking his troubles away,
The flowering queen,
And the queenly flowers,
All making the emperor's day

Pure and Peaceful Song (number 3)

She walks through the peonies,
Glistening with dew,
The smell of those flowers is
Wonderful too,
Lucky to be the emperor!

No need to yearn,

For a fairy companion,

To spirit his life away,

Of all queens in history,

Who could match her in beauty?

Today, or indeed, any day?

They would all need to take up,

So much new make up,

Including Yang Guifei

Notes

Li Bai was summoned to the Emperor's garden, a great honour. He was told to bring a poem to the empress. This gave him some difficulty, for virtually no-one had seen the Empress. Also, Li Bai could not say she was immortal; that was the emperor's role. He also had to be wary of any comparison he made. He solved it, in the first poem, by locating her in semi mythical places used by the gods. By the time the request came for a second and third poem, Li Bai was getting fed up.

It shows in the poetry. In the final lines he contrasts the empress with Fei Wei, a previous empress. Jealous voices in the palace convinced the empress that the poem insulted her. She asked for Li Bai's head. The emperor agreed. Saner voices at the palace convinced the emperor to commute the sentence to banishment, which duly happened. Li Bai's supporters convinced the emperor that he wouldn't want to be known, in the future, as the emperor who slew China's greatest poet.

Thoughts on a Quiet Night
by Li Bai

Before my bed bright moonlight shines,

Perhaps there's frost upon the ground,

I raise my head to see the moon,

Thinking of home, I lay back down.

☀

Notes

This is probably Li Bai's most famous poem. Almost every Chinese kid learns this off by heart. It is on the subject of homesickness.

Endlessly Yearning to be in Changgan

by Li Bai

Crickets click on an autumn night,
By the golden railings of the well,
I see sparkling frost which makes
My bamboo mat look cold and chill.

My only lamp looks dull and old,
I want my thoughts to cease and die,
Roll back the curtain to see the moon,
Vainly heaving one long sigh.

She is beautiful, my blossom,
Beyond the clouds and far away,
Above, the black night of heaven,
Below, green waters ebb and sway.

It's a long way to reach my heaven,
Whither my spirit bitterly flies,
Along remote and distant roads,

Making its way to paradise.

The faraway mountains cannot be crossed,
Endlessly yearning, my heart is lost.

☀

Notes

Li Bai was exiled by the emperor for insulting the empress. See 'Pure and Peaceful Song'.

Changgan was the ancient capital of China, where the poet wanted to be. The beautiful blossom that is beyond reach is a position in government, for which he yearns. But even his spirit cannot take him there.

Hard Walking on the Road
by Li Bai

Lovely wine from a golden cup,
Ten thousand coins to fill the jug,
Tasty food served on jade platters,
Ten thousand more, what does it matter?
I stop drinking, chopsticks aside,
Sword in hand I look all around,

What should I do, what should I do?
But from my heart, nothing is found.
I want to cross the Yellow River,
Because of ice, I just can't go,
I want to climb the Taihang mountain,
But Taihang is cloaked in snow.
I like to go fishing in the streams,
So, I take my boat beyond the sun,
It only happens in my dreams,
Hard walking on the road!
Hard walking on the road!
So many crossings on the way,
Which is the right path to take?
One day I'll sail straight to the sea,
Crash through the great waves, my boat and me.

Joking with Du Fu
by Li Bai

At the top of Little Rice Mountain,
I chanced to meet Du Fu,
In the midday sun he was wearing,
A rain hat made out of bamboo,
"Pray tell me sir", I then asked him,
"Why you've got such a scrawny frame?
Is it caused by the hardship of writing,
Those painful poems again?"

☀

Notes

Li Bai and Du Fu were friends and admired each other's poetry. Du Fu was known to be tall and very thin.

Waking up Drunk on a Spring Day, Talking about Aspirations

by Li Bai

Life is an endless dream,
Here in this world of ours,
In work or stress or toil,
I'm not going to spend my hours,
And so, I was legless, all day,
On the porch outside the front door,
I very slowly came round,
Sprawled, as I was, on the floor,
My eyes focused first on the yard,
I stared at a solitary bird,
Chirping amongst the flowers,
The oriole's singing was heard,
The song reached me on Spring breezes,
As I asked "What is the season?"
Moved, I poured me a cup of wine,
Wine was still there, that's my reason,
Whilst waiting for the moon to rise,
I belted out a sweet refrain,

By the time I reached the last verse,
Would you believe it? Sloshed again!

Marble Steps Complaint
by Li Bai

Marble steps turn white with dew,
Through the long night,
My socks soak through,
I let the crystal curtain fall,
The autumn moon is
An exquisite view

Saying Goodbye to Librarian Shu Yun at Xie Tiao tower

by Li Bai

Yesterday, you abandoned me,
Past times I can't preserve,
Yesterday, I was abandoned,
All my thoughts disturbed.

In autumn, wild geese fly for days,
Strong winds take them miles away,
I take in the view from here,
Go upstairs, and drink, and stay.

Your writings are both strong and clear,
Like those old poets of the Han,
My poems are like Xiao Xie's,
Very easy to understand.

There are things we want to do,
Reach for the sky, and touch the moon,
Cut the water with your sword,

You'll never stop the river flowing.

I raise my cup, my sorrows I'll drown,
But the problem gets worse, as the liquor goes down,

Let's face it, many things have no solution,
The world frustrates without resolution,
So, tomorrow, I'll go out on my boat,
Let my hair down and drift, afloat.

Notes

Xiao Xie is pronounced as *Shh ow!* and *She eh.*

Sitting Alone on Jingting Mountain
by Li Bai

Birds flock high, away they fly,
A small cloud drifts, alone in the sky,
Not tiring of our company,
We gaze at each other,
Jingting and me.

The Farewell Pavilion
by Li Bai

This is the place, under heaven,
The saddest place to say goodbye,
This is the Lao Lao pavilion,
This is where sad hearts will die,
The willow branch no longer blooms,
Spring breezes only tell the gloom
of parting.

Gazing at the Waterfall at Lu Mountain, Far Away
by Li Bai

On Xianglu mountain,
The sun is shining,
Purple mist rising,
Seen from afar.
A crystal curtain,
Hangs from the mountain,
So very distant,

So very high,
One thousand metres,
from top to bottom,
A Milky Way falling,
Out of the sky.

Notes

Modern Lushan, next to Xiangin (pronounced *She ang in*) mountain is still a tourist attraction in the Jiangxi province.

To Meng Haoran
by Li Bai

Love you, Meng the master,
Admired the world over,
For your words like pearls,
And high moral standards,
When you were young
You gave up cap and carriage,
When you grew old
You went into the forest,
With your rosy cheeks
And mop of white hair,
Drinking under the sky
By the moon's bright glare,
Flowers there, to beguile you,
No ruler controlled you,
Often out on a spree,
Always calm and adored
By the people and me,
You are a towering peak,
And when you speak,

Your words are the clean breeze
Coming down from the mountain,
I bow before them,
I bow before you.

Notes

Cap and carriage are the trappings of a court official.

To Wang Lun
by Li Bai

On the ferry at Peach Flower lake,
My wistful farewells I'm ready to make,
Then you, and your comrades, appear,
Your singing and stamps fill the air,
Let me tell you this, my Wang Lun,
I don't care if the lake is deep,
Deeper than any sea,
That lake will never be deeper,
Than your deep love for me.

Remembering Qin E
by Li Bai

The flute plays so sadly,
Sounds like someone crying,
Qin E awakes
From her sad dreaming,
With the moon in the sky
Hanging over her dwelling,
Every year on green willow,
The same moon is shining.

On the bridge at Baling,
She recalls the sad parting,
The double ninth feast
At Leyouyuan starting,
No replies to Xianyang,
No replies were forthcoming
Only the West wind
Was softly blowing.

Only the West wind
Was softly blowing,
At sunset, at night,
The sun was still glowing
On Han tombs and palaces
Which were still standing,
While Qin E recalls
Her own sad dreaming.

Notes

Qin E is pronounced *chin eh*. Leyouyuan is pronounced *Le* (as in the French Le) *yo you en*. Xian is pronounced *she en*.

The double ninth festival is, traditionally, a time for family reunions.

Seeing off Meng Haoran at the Yellow Crane Tower

by Li Bai

From Yellow Crane Tower

My old friend has to go.

Willow flowers in the March mists,

He is bound for Yangzhou,

His lone sail vanishes into the blue,

Where the Chang jiang goes,

So must he too.

☀

Notes

Yellow crane tower is in Wuhan, a famous tourist attraction which was rebuilt after a fire.
    Yangzhou, pronounced *yang joe*, is, like Wuhan, a town on the Yangtze river. *Chang jiang* means Big River and is the Yangtze river.

Sweet Rain on a Spring Night
by Du Fu

Good rain knows when
is the best time for coming,
Arriving in Spring when
Everything's growing,
Bringing rain in the night, softly,
Soaking the earth, silently,
Black clouds over roads through meadows,
On the river, boats' lanterns glow,
See, the red flowers glisten with dew,
Blossoming everywhere, here in Chengdu.

Soldiers and Carts on the Road to War(to the tune of)

by Du Fu

On the road you can hear carriages creaking,
You can also hear some people weeping,
Each soldier carries his arrows and bow,
Each parent and child watching them go,
Horses whinnying, carrying loads,
People stop soldiers by grabbing their coats,
Their anguished cries to heaven are raised,
Xianyang bridge is obscured by haze,
Passers by ask, what is happening now?
The rulers take all the men, they avow,
They join the army, at fifteen, and thenceforth,
They go to defend the lands to the North,
When they reach forty, they must then go West,
To grow and tend crops to feed all the rest,
They plaited their hair at Li Zheng's orders.
Now, with grey hair, they still defend borders,
There, at the border, blood flows like tides,
Land grabbing goes on, the ruler decides,

There are strong women who are left behind,
With little to harvest from their daily grind,
Soldiers, in this war, hard fighting endure,
Like chickens or dogs, pushed to the floor,
This winter, Qin soldiers fight without rest,
And old men ask how can they protest?
Governors hurry to bring in the rent,
But who can pay taxes when the money's all spent?
People don't want sons, just daughters
Who grow up and get married,
Don't go off to be slaughtered,
Haven't you seen the bones of the dead.
At Qing Hai lake, thrown round the edge?
Old ghosts weep softly, new ghosts loudly wail,
On cloudy, rain filled nights, their cries prevail.
In the East of Qin are two hundred states,
Thousands of villages left to their fate,
In abandoned fort and abandoned field,
Weeds and wild grass, the only yield.

Docking Near Feng Jiao Bridge at Night

by Zhang Ji

The moon is climbing down the sky,

Crows are cawing, passing by,

And it's so chilly at night,

Difficult to catch a nap,

Watching maples on the bank,

On other boats are waving lights,

From my vessel, near Suzhou's walls,

I hear the Hanshan temple's bells.

Strolling by the River, Alone, Looking at the Flowers

by Du Fu

On Huang Siniang's plants
Are so many flowers,
Almost cov'ring the path
That goes by her bower,
There are thousands of blooms,
Weighing down branches,
Butterflies darting,
In quick easy dances,
An oriole calling,
Happily singing,
Calm and relaxing,
Sharing the feeling
That this pleasant moment
Around us, is bringing.

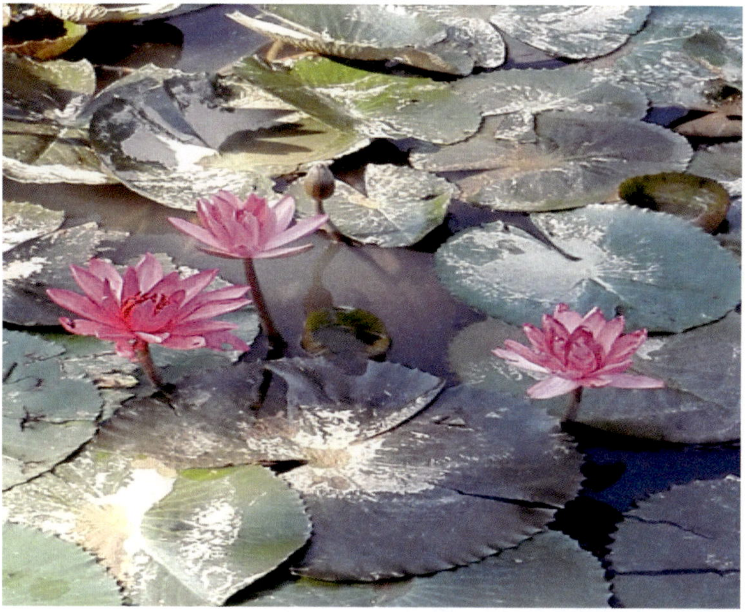

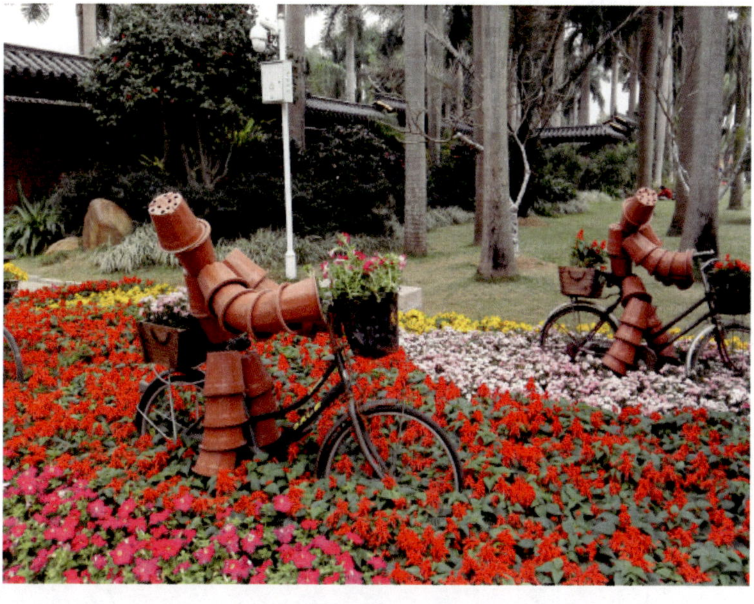

Feeling Sorry for the Farmer
by Li Shen

Sweat is falling upon the ground,

Hoeing under a blazing sun,

Of all the food left in your bowl,

A grain of rice shows hard work done.

☀

Notes

This is an admonition for all children to eat up their food. Every kid learns this rhyme.

Poem Finished in Seven Steps
by Cao Zhi

Bean stalks burn to boil the beans,
One bean in the pot is heard to shout
"From the same root came the two of us,
Why so eager to snuff me out?"

Notes

Cao Pi was emperor of Wei. He told his brother Cao Zhi to write a poem, after taking seven steps only. Cao Pi was worried that his brother would try to usurp the throne so he set him what he thought was an impossible task. This is the successful poem. Cao Pi spared his brother.

Song of the Departing Son
by Meng Jiao

The kind mother's hand holds the thread,
For her son, she is making new clothes,
Later, no-one will make repairs,

She makes them strong, she mends and sews,
She worries that soon he'll depart,
Why not return the love in her heart?
How do the first grasses of Spring
Repay the Spring sunshine for what it brings?

A Lyre
by Su Shi

Some say that the tune
Comes from the lyre, but
Why doesn't it play
When the box lid is shut?

Some say that the tune
Is in the player's fingers,
Your hands are here,
And no music lingers!

Autumn Moon
by Su Shi

Raising my glass, I ask the blue sky,
How long before the new moon rises?
They don't know, in heaven's places,
What the day or what the year is.
I want to go riding on the wind,
Riding up to heaven anew,
Yet still I fear the jade moon palace,
And I fear jade railings too.
Those who are dwellers upon high,
Don't know the coldness of the sky,
Uniquely, in the world of men,
My shadow and I go dancing by.
The moon moves round the red pavilion,
Weaving through the curtained door,
Shining on the sleepless ones,
Who should not pine for evermore.
Why does the full moon always shine,
On those who are separated?
And why, since ancient times

Are facts like this always debated?
People have meetings and partings,
To add to their joy and sorrow,
The moon can be dark or bright,
It can wax or wane tomorrow.
For countless years we wished by the moon,
Wishfully hoping, hopeless for ever,
Now, divided by a thousand miles,
We watch the same fair moon together.

Notes

Jade moon palace, where the gods live, is above the sky.

Remembering Events at Red Cliff (to the tune of Charming Nian Nu)

by Su Shi

The Great River flows to the East,
Washing away memories
Of brave heroes of the past.
Go west from ancient ruins,
Beyond old fortifications,
Until you reach Red Cliff, at last.

Giant rocks reach skyward in serried ranks,
Massive waves crash upon river banks,
Foam looking like heaps of snow,
The vista is beautiful and wild,
Like some old painting we all know.

I reminisce about that year,
How many warriors battled there?
Imagining the brave Zhou Yu,
Recently married to Xiao Qiao, too.

He laughs and jokes with his new bride,
His behaviour is chivalrous,
His demeanour courteous,
As on the waters soldiers died.

In his hand, a feather fan,
A silken headscarf for the man,
As entire battleships are burned.
I recall the ancient fighting,
As I remember the age old scenes,
My soul full of feeling for
All the battles that had been.
Whereas, I laugh at myself,
Indeed there are those
Who would laugh at me,
With my early grey hair,
And my poetry.
I reflect that life is but a dream,
As I drink to the bright moon over the stream.

Notes

The battle of the Red Cliff was a decisive battle at the end of the Han dynasty, 208 A.D. It was fought between the Southern warlords and Cao Cao whose forces were numerically superior. Only the Yangtze river separated the two armies. I say "only", but in fact it is over a kilometre wide in places and has its own reefs and currents. In the poem it is described as the Great River.

General Zhou Yu (pronounced *Joe yoo*), with 50,000 troops defeated Cao Cao's army of 800, 000, and used fire ships to destroy Cao's fleet and the on board soldiers. The Chinese film Red Cliff is pretty good too, 2008, directed by John Wu. Su Shi's famous poem was written some 800 years later. The truth is that no one really knows where the battle took place. Three Kingdoms refers to one of China's four great classical novels. Three kingdoms is in four volumes. If you can read it to the end, well done! Xiao Qiao is pronounced show to rhyme with now, ciao as in the Italian way.

On the New City Road
by Su Shi

On the New City road,
And the East Wind knows,
I am going up
Into the mountains.

It blows away the clouds
As it breaks the sounds
Of rain on roofs,
On this outing.
The now white clouds look like hats
Upon the peaks,
And the early morning sun,
Like a big copper ball,
Over the tree line peeps.

In the open countryside,
I appreciate the sight,
Of a wild peach tree,

With a smile,
Growing next to
A short bamboo fence,
It's blossoming in style.

In the pure water of the bubbling brook,
The sand at the bottom, you can see,
And on the bank, swaying in the breeze,
The beautiful willow trees,
West mountain happy families are the very best,
They cook mallow and bamboo shoots,
For the ploughmen, when they rest.

Impromptu Poem
by Su Shi

I am a sick old man,
Wasting time alone,
Loosely, on the frosty wind,
My white beard is blown.
My cheery red face,
Kidded a little kid,
I'm smiling, for, my ruddy cheeks,
Are down to the booze I did!

A Joke for Zhang Xian
by Su Shi

The bride is eighteen, the young man eighty,
A mop of white hair next to a red nightie,
Like the love birds sewn on the quilt,
They became a couple that night,
Crab apple pink topped by pear blossom white!

Notes

His friend Zhang Xian (pronounced *Jang she an*) was marrying a much younger girl. He was 80, she was 18.

Zhang Xian's 65-year-old son attended the wedding. They went on to have 3 children. Zhang Xian said that his only regret was not marrying at 70.

To His Dead Wife
by Su Shi

She died ten endless years ago,
Ten boundless years, and so,
I don't often think about her,
She's impossible to forget,
A thousand li to her cold plot,
And I can't tell my loneliness.

She wouldn't know me, if we met now,
My dust smeared face and frosted brow,

In the deep night, sleeping, I roam,
ND Dreams take me back to our old home,
By the little window, she dresses,
Doing her make-up, tieing her tresses,
Wordlessly, at each other we stare,
Too many flowing tears are there.

I expect, every year, I must

Go back to that heart rending place,

Where the pine trees stand lonely guard,

And light from the new moon plays.

Notes

A li is about half a kilometre. When his wife died, Su Shi planted pine nuts all around her grave. The growing trees would protect the occupant of the grave from evil spirits.

Written on the Wall of Xilin Monastery

by Su Shi

Sideways, you see a mountain range,

A mountain facing you,

Seen from near, seen from afar,

Always a diff'rent view,

Seen from on high or from below,

A changing vista too,

I can't tell you much about Mount Lushan,

Maybe because that's where I am,

Upon it!

Poem to Li Bai
by Du Fu

After we parted, I looked around,

Not knowing where I should go,

Aimlessly drifting like wind-blown flowers,

We said sorry to Ge Hong,

Failing to find the elixir of life.

Now I'm drinking, and not stopping,

And drinking happily, I say,

I drink to fill the lonely time,

On each and every lonely day,

Failing to find the elixir of life,

What use a bold spirit?

An Invitation to Liu Shijiu
Bai Juyi

Green foam on new cloudy wine,
A red clay stove to keep us warm,
Later tonight, there may be snow,
Will you drink with me?
Yes or no?

To the Tune of "The Beauty of Yu"

by Li Yu

When will the time of Spring flowers be over?

How much can be recalled of those past delights?

When will the time of the full moon be done?

When the East wind filled my attic, last night?

Sadness prevents me recalling my homeland,

Stops me rememb'ring my enduring love,

And the full moon shines in the sky so brightly,

Beaming down from the heavens above.

Carved railings and jade steps must all still be there,

Young looking faces, all changed, at least,

Ask me to describe how much I despair,

I'll point to Spring waters and floods flowing East.

☼

Notes

The emperor Li Yu had been deposed. He had been supplied with poison in his prison cell, in a very Socratic manner. This was the last poem he wrote, it is still sung to this day, a very haunting song.

The reference to carved railings and jade steps is a reference to heaven, where he will join his ancestors.

Buying Peonies (to the Tune of "Buddhist Dancers")

by Bai Juyi

It's the end of Spring,

Many carthorses seen, going here and there,

It's really crowded, everywhere,

The peonies are blooming now,

And it's the custom in Chang'an town,

The rich all flock to buy fresh blooms.

Prices, here, are never shown,

That depends on the type,

The peonies, here, are so very fresh,

The colour of blood falling down,

Kept in sheds, with fences all round,

Five bolts of white cloth cost less

Than a small bunch of flowers,

With soil round their roots,

Well watered too,

They look as new

As the day they were picked.

Every home has to have some,

A family tradition,
For people to gaze on,
They don't think it's a luxury.
In the place where these flowers are sold,
A poor farmer, by chance, passes by,
He lowers his head and heaves a sigh,
Who cares about this or why?
The taxes paid in a year, by ten middle class families,
Are less than the price of a bunch of dark peonies.

Harem Poem
by Bai Juyi

Her thin handkerchief
Is wet with her tears,
Her dreams have been crushed,
At night she hears,
The beat of the music
From the palace, at the front.
Pretty and young,
She isn't yet old,
Just not in favour,

Left out in the cold,
She leans against
The fragrant urn,
Sits through the night,
Waits for the Dawn

Arrogant Eunuchs
by Bai Juyi

The finest riding outfits
Can be seen on chubby horses,
With vain and haughty manners,
They are spreading across the roads,
Sumptuous horse decorations,
Spotted with tiny flecks of dust,
So, I ask a passer by
Who and what these people are,
The answer is they're eunuchs,
Men who serve the emperor,
Red ribbons for court officials,
Purple ones adorn the generals,
All showing off their positions,

All heading for the barracks,
All rushing off for a feast,
Passing by like scudding clouds,
Finest wines to fill their tables,
And, choicest and rarest foods
Coming from the land and sea,
Tangerines brought from Dongting,
With fish fillets straight from Tianchi,
When their appetites are sated,
They feel they deserve their feast,
And, when they have drunk their fill,
They show no restraint at all,
Yet this year, there is a bad drought,
South of the Yangtze river,
Starving men eat each other.

The Old Serving Maid in the Palace
by Bai Juyi

This is the Shangyang palace,
There is the serving maid,
Her skin is getting darker,
Her hair already greyed,
The palace gate is guarded
By eunuchs dressed in green,
The gate is always closed,
How many Springs has she seen?
Selected for the court at sixteen,
Sixty now and in time frozen,
She is the last remaining one,
Of the hundred that were chosen,
To friends and family she said goodbye,
And, in the carriage, refused to cry,
"Go to the palace!" they all said,
"Be spoiled by the emperor, instead."

Her face like lilies in a glade,
Her breasts as white as any jade,
She couldn't wait to be seen,
And seen she was, by concubine Yang,
And sent, in secret, to Shangyang,
Her whole life spent in one lonely room,
Sleepless in the Autumn gloom,
Waiting for the dawn, at last, to come,
Her candle casts shadows on the wall,
From her window, she hears the rain fall,
Spring is also passing by,
She sits alone, stares at the sky,
In the palace orioles sing,
But these birds just do not please her,
Swallows nest and fly together,
She is old, and no-one sees her.
Swallows and orioles migrate,
The palace is cold and desolate,
Spring goes suddenly, and then,
Everywhere, Autumn again,
She doesn't know how many years go by,
By day the palace, by night the sky,

She knows the sunrise in the East,
She knows the sunset in the West,
Five hundred full and sickle moons,
But this old lady never rests,
High official is the name they gave her,
And still no-one to seek her favour,
With her old fashioned shoes,
And clothes that fit tightly,
Her old fashioned make-up
Would be seen as unsightly,
If she dared to venture outside,
People would then recognize,
The fashion from the bygone time
Of the old ruler Xuan Zong.

The people trapped in the palace,
Suffer now, have suffered long,
From youth to old age, then left to rot,
Impossible to change, so what?
If you see the painting called "Beauties",
Produced for the official Lu Shang,
Then, you've seen the white haired old lady,
Trapped in the palace they call Shangyang.

Notes

Emperor Xuan Zong (*Shoo en zong*) 685 – 762. It was towards the end of his reign that the girl was sent to his court to be a concubine.

Yang Guifei, 719-756, the emperor's favourite concubine, made sure the emperor never saw the girl. Ruthless and ambitious, she had been his son's wife till the emperor divorced them and took her as his concubine.

Shangyang, is one of the emperor's palaces and far from Xi'an, the then capital. Situated in modern Luoyang.

Lu Shang, the emperor's chancellor, used to commission portraits of prospective concubines and the emperor would select the ones he fancied and they would then be summoned, in industrial quantities. It is clear that this system revolted Bai Juyi, as it did many other poets. Most poets wrote about the sadness of the girl's lives.

Drinking and Looking at the Peonies

by Liu Yuxi

Today is my day for a sup,
Whilst facing the peonies,
Happy to drink many cups,

I worry that the buds are saying,
"For the old, we won't open up".

Homecoming After Work
by Anonymous

I joined the army, aged fifteen,
Eighty when I returned at last,
On my way I met a neighbor,
"Anyone at home?" I asked.
"See for yourself, your house is there!"
Where mature cypresses and pines,
Grow around all the gravestones,
Where rabbits through dog holes walk in line.

Pheasants fly through exposed roof beams,
Wild rice is growing in the yard,
I use my pestle to remove the rice husks,
Because I know they are very hard.

Wild mallow from around the well,
I use, with rice, to make my feast,

There is no-one to share my food,
I go out the gate and look to the East,
My tears have soaked my clothes.

Notes

The title, like the poem, is understated. Sixty five years as a soldier is merely referred to as work.

It was the custom to plant seeds from evergreen trees around graves to protect the dead. See Su Shi's poem To His Dead Wife'. House dogs could leave the houseyard walled area via a small hole under a wall. Mallow is still used today as an infusion.

The Complaint in Spring
by Liu Fangping

Through her window and net curtains,
She watches the sun as it's setting,
In her splendid golden mansion,
She notes the approaching evening,
No one to see her in this place,
Traces of tears lining her face,

The courtyard is deserted,
Pear blossoms cover the floor,
For her, Spring is almost over,
No-one to try the yard door.

Notes

This is a poem about a sad concubine who vainly waits for the emperor's call. We can tell that the mansion was owned by the emperor by the reference to golden. The colour yellow was reserved for the emperor. The concubine's status was reflected in the quality of her dwelling. The fact that she is housed in a mansion indicates that she was once held in esteem.

Bird Cries From the Ravine
by Wang Wei

Nothing better to do at all,
Here on a lonely mountainside,
I watch osmanthus blossoms fall,
The spring evening is calm and clear,
That is, until the moon appears,

Startling the birds in the ravine,
Fitfully heard
The cries of birds

Jottings
by Wang Wei

You've come from my home town!
You must know everything
That's happening!
The plum tree by my front window,
On the day you left,
Was it blossoming?

The Goose Chant
by Luo Bin Wang

Goosey! Goosey! Goosey!

Bend your neck up!

Sing to the sky!

White feathers float

On the clear water,

Red paddles send ripples,

As you pass by

Sent North on a Rainy Night

by Li Shang Yin

You ask and I don't know,
When will I come back again?
The pools upon Ba Shan mountain,
Fill with the steady night rain,
I wonder when we will trim the candles,
As we sit, by the west window,
I wonder when we will talk together,
Of Ba Shan's rains' incessant flow?

To the Tune "Slow Tunes" (written after her husband died)

by Li Qing Zhao

I have searched hard, in my distress,
In vain, I feel alone, depressed,
It's hard to care for myself,
And hard to get a decent rest.

In Autumn, the weather changes,
In the evening, the cold wind blows,
Even after a couple of glasses,
How can I tolerate the cold?

Today, wild geese were passing by,
I feel sad, they are friends of mine.

Fallen blossoms litter the yard,
From the old chrysanthemum tree,
They are withered, they have faded,
Who will clear them up for me?

Sitting at my window alone,
Waiting for the night to come,
It is dusk and now it's raining,
I hear raindrops gently falling,
On the leaves of the parasol tree,
Taking in all that's before me,
One word is not enough, misery.

Tipsy
by Li Qingzhao

There are black clouds filling the sky,
My sadness is just like the mist
That drifts, and covers all the ground,
Incense falls lazily
From the golden beast censer,
The double ninth feast again comes round.

My bed is veiled by curtains,
On jade pillows I rest my head,
The cold still creeps in at midnight,
And I lie freezing on my bed.

Next to yellow flowers, I was drinking,
Till dusk, that's how my time was spent,
And now my sleeves have the smell of blossoms,
All the chrysanthemums' heady scent.
Don't tell me late autumn can't make me sad,
At the window, in the evening hours,
When the west wind shakes the curtain,
I will have faded like the flowers.

Plums Fall Down
by Anonymous

Plums are falling down,
But most stay on the tree,
Young man, make your proposal,
Please say you do want me!
This could be our lucky day,
So, tell me now, and don't delay!

Plums are falling down,
But some stay on the tree,
Young man, make your proposal,
Please say you do want me!
This could be our lucky day,
Don't waste our time and don't delay!

Use your basket to collect
The fruit that's fallen from the tree,
Young man, make your proposal,
Please say you do want me!
So tell me now, and please, don't wait!
Stop dithering, don't hesitate!

☀

Notes

The young lady is very aware of the passing of time (shown in the falling of plums) and the effect on her chances of finding love. Her tone, though polite, increases in stridency from verse to verse until the final line which reveals a degree of frustration. For comparison see the poem by Robert Herrick, *To the Virgins, to Make Much of Time.*

Looking at the Moon and Missing Those I Care About who are Far Away

by Zhang Jiuling

The Ocean separates you from me,

As the bright moon rises, out of the sea,

People, like me, hate these long nights,

Sleepless, I think of the ones who love me,

I blow out the candle to savour the moonlight,

I feel it's cold, put on my clothes,

Can't show you how lovely or even how bright,

The only way to share its lovely beams,

Is when I can share them, in my dreams.

Listening to the Zither
by Li Duan

She faces the jade bridge,
On her exquisite zither,
Beautiful notes
Come from the white hands
Of the sweet lady who
Is playing the zither.
To see if she can find a man,
As discerning as Gentleman Zhou,
In the middle of the piece she is playing,
A planned, deliberate, wrong note,
Comes from the exquisite zither.

☀

Notes

Zhou (pronounced *Joe*) was a famous general who really appreciated good music and would have recognised the deliberate error and pointed it out. So, the wrong note played was designed to attract the attention of any man who was a music lover and would appreciate her playing. The jade bridge is the bridge on the instrument.

Crossing the Han River
by Song Zhiwen

Winter has passed, it's almost Spring,
No news from my home in Ling Wai,
The closer I get to my home,
The more I want to cry,
All I want is a little news,
I daren't even ask the passersby.

Notes

Ling Wai is the modern Ling Nan in Guangdong province.

Drinking Wine
by Tao Yuanming

I live in a city, without remorse,
I can't hear the noise from cart or horse,
So, ask me how I can escape that scene?
My soul is distant, calm, serene,
In my mind there is nothing but peace,
As I pick daisies, by the fence to the East.
I notice the South hills, far, far away,
The mountain smells reach me anew,
It's really quite pleasant, everywhere, now,
The scents in the evening, the beautiful view,
Birds are returning to their nests,
Everything here is of life's best,
I can't explain it properly,
The feelings I cannot express.

In Memoriam
by Tao Yuanming

You have your birth, then you have nought,
Yet early death doesn't make life short,
Only last night, you were still living,
Now, a note in the book of the ghost king,
Your body lies in its coffin, at last,
Who knows when your spirit passed?
Young kids contemplate death and cry,
Good friends are mourning where you lie,
The dead can't tell a gift from a loss,
If there's right or wrong, gold or dross,
In many years' time, at the end of the story,
Who will care less if there's shame or glory?
The real regret is that during your time,
You hadn't the chance to drink enough wine

Notes

There was no heaven, only hell. It was ruled by the Ghost King. Once he had your name in his little book, you were his forever. Sometimes he would refuse to enter your details. In that case you would go back to the land of the living. The author wrote this and died two months later.

`Delayed Return from Shu`
by Zhang Yue

My return from Shu has been delayed,
And my welcome overstayed,
I really want to get back soon!
My heart flies faster than sun or moon,
 I really want to get back soon!
All my plans already thwarted,
And my journey not yet started,
The harsh Autumn wind brooks no delay,
It must be in Luoyang today,
Before I get leave to go away.

`Notes`

Shu is the modern Sichuan province. Luoyang is in the West of Henan province and was formerly a capital of China for thirteen dynasties.

To the Tune of "Song of a Bamboo Branch"

by Liu Yuxi

The mountain is full of red peach blossoms,

As the waters of Shu lap on the shore,

His love, like red flowers, fades oh so easily,

My grief, like the river, flows evermore.

Rural Scene by the River Wei
by Wang Wei

The light, at sunset, shines on the village,
Herds of cows and sheep come back down the lane,
A granddad, who's missing his grandson, waits,
With his stick in hand, he stands by the gate,
Pheasants are calling out from the paddy fields,
Telling their friends, the new crop is growing,
Silkworms are sleeping, wrapped in their cocoons,
Dozing and happy, after eating their food,
Peasants, with hoes, back home are returning,
Meeting together, laughing and joking,
I envy their life, so quiet and soothing,
"Going back home" is the song that I'm singing.

Notes

The song he sings is called Shi Wei, which is actually a poem in a collection of old poems. The Wei River flows from Niaoshu mountain in Gansu province.

Upset in the West Palace in Autumn

by Wang Changling

A lotus flower is less pretty

Than her artfully made up face,

From the emperor's boat comes the scent,

Of hair with jade and pearl graced,

No-one sees she is sad,

Hid behind her wide fan,

Vainly she waits,

Waits for the man,

To appear.

Hoping for the king to arrive,

Is like snatching the moon from the sky.

Your Behaviour in Your Youth
by Wang Wei

An important official
Worked for a great general,
Being given a knight's role,
Without a complaint,
You obeyed your orders,
Fought hard at the borders,
At Yuyang fierce fighting
Never minding the pain,
Death, for you, was not a worry,
Only white bones now tell the story.

The Cock is Crowing (from the Shi Jing)
by Anonymous

"Hey, the cock is crowing!
People are going to court,"
"It's only bluebottles buzzing,
It's really nothing at all,"

"Hey, in the East, I can see the daylight!"
"Nah, it's just the moon, shining bright!"
"Insects are coming,
Happy to share their dreams with you!"
"Hey, the meeting's over,
Officials are streaming away,
Hope that they won't hate you,
For not being there today!"

☀

Notes

This is an early morning conversation, between a man and his partner. To separate the two speakers, we have used inverted commas and started the partner's speeches with "Hey". The man is an official of some kind and supposed to attend court at dawn and he's finding reasons not to go. He decides to get up when it is too late. Equally, his partner wants him to go to work!

Seeing West Lake from the Wanghu Pavilion
by Su Shi
(written after heavy drinking)

Black clouds like ink spills,
Not hiding the hills,
Spattering the boats,
White raindrops, like pearls.

The wind, crossing the plain,
Disperses the clouds,
The vast waters of West lake,
Go flowing by,
From Wanghu pavilion,
And then meet the sky.

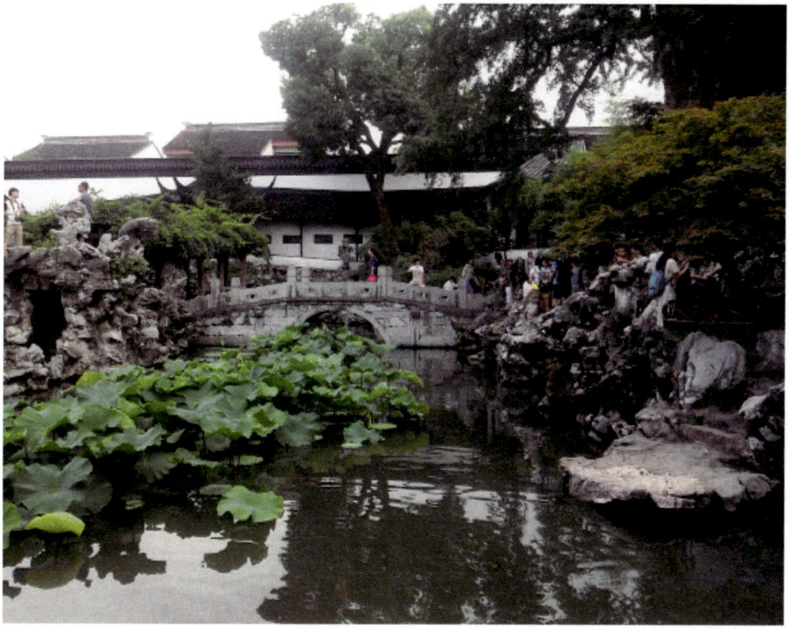

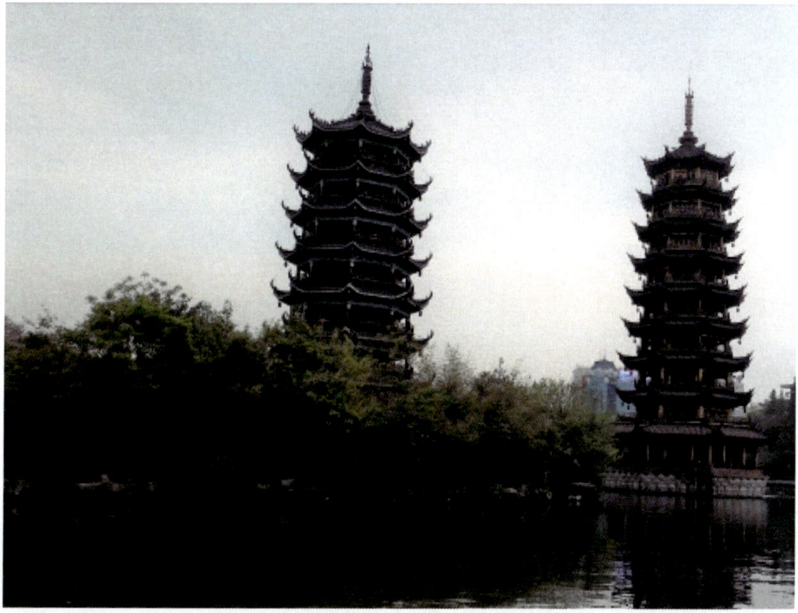

Drove my Carriage
by Anonymous

Drove my carriage up to the East Gate,
And see the North Cemetery from afar,
North of the city, I see many graves,
There, poplars are bending in the wind,
Pine and cypress trees grow along the road
On both sides and look so scary to me.

In the graves, corpses, in the dark, always,
Sleeping by yellow, underground streams,
Never to wake up again,

Time passes by, like East flowing waters,
Life is as brief as the morning dew,
Life is hurried, like a hotel stay,
And not as stable as gold or rock,
People live and die across generations,
The rich, also subject to this rule,
Which they can't alter, much as they try,
They take elixirs and try to be gods,

And are often cheated by medicines,

Why not taste delicious spirits instead?

Put on pretty clothes and enjoy your lives!

Missing my Shandong Brothers at Double Ninth Festival

by Wang Wei

A wanderer, I live alone,

Missing my relatives, far from home,

As any festival approaches,

I think they will climb the mountain,

Today, each one wearing

A sprig of dogwood, in his hair,

And I'm not there.

Notes

Traditionally, the Double Ninth Festival is a time for family reunions and remembering those who can't be with you. The sprig of dogwood is to remember absent friends.

To Li Dan and Yuan Xi
by Wei Yingwu

Last year, we met amongst the flowers,
Parting, they were still in bloom,
Another year has passed since then,
Flowers are blooming once again.
Human affairs are limitless,
Difficult to assess or guess,
Now, in Spring, I worry in secret,
And every night I sleep alone,
I think about my homeland fields,
And the refugees that fill the town.
My illnesses still cause me pain,
I am ashamed to take my pay.
Someone said you would visit me,
At the West tower, I'll wait for you,
Just hoping that you will come soon,
How many times will I watch the moon?

Yearning for Home
by Yu Guangzhou

When I was young,
Homesickness was a small stamp,
On one side my mother,
Me on the other.

When I grew up,
Homesickness was a ticket for a boat ride,
Me, on this side,
On the other my bride.

And later on,
Homesickness was a mound on a grave,
Me outside,
My mother inside.
And now,
Homesickness is a shallow strait,
I am here,
My motherland is over there.

Notes

The writer left Guangzhou at an early age to move to Taiwan but he still felt Chinese in himself. Taiwan is separated from mainland China by a narrow stretch of water.

Song of Chu Sai
by Wang Chang Ling

It is, still, the same old moon,
And the same old practices
Are being handed down,
Through Qing and Han dynasties,
We, the soldiers, were ordered to march,
And had thousands of miles to go,
We, the soldiers, fighting the enemy,
Never returning to our homes,
The generals in Dragon city.
If they were still alive,
On Yunshan hills, they would've stopped
The Hu's relentless Eastern drive.

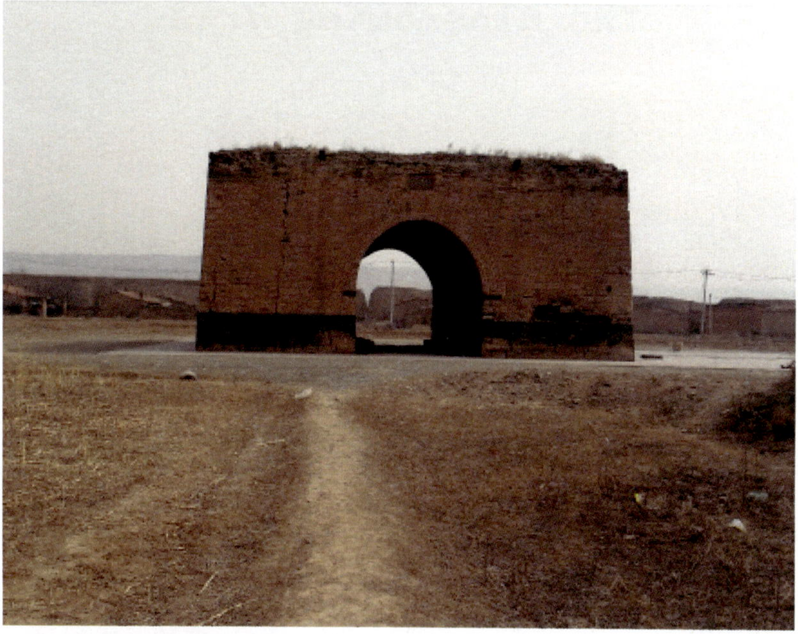

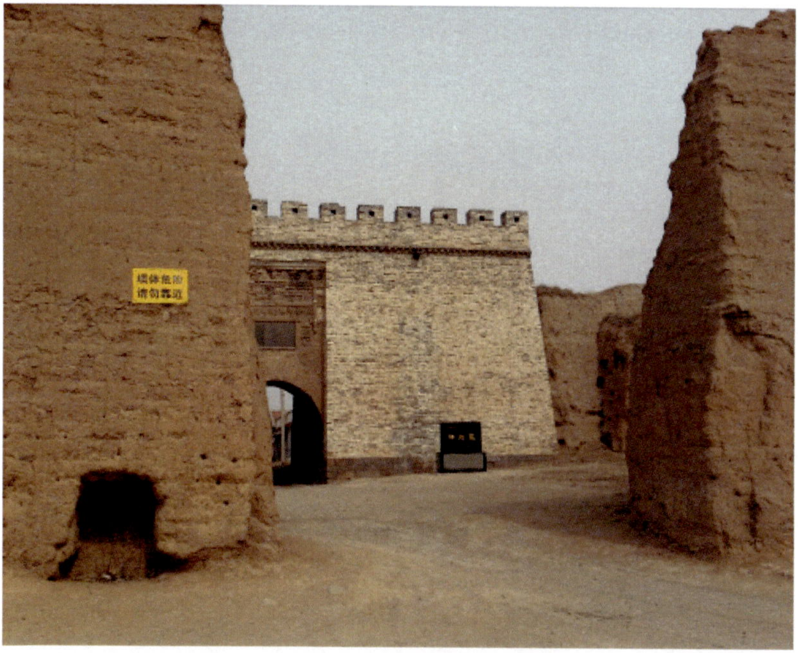

The Blossoming Tree
by Xi Murong

I prayed to Buddha for five hundred years,
I prayed to him to let you see me
At my most beautiful hour,
Buddha turned me into a tree.
You walk by me, and on this day,
My tree is flowering, on your way.
Every bloom marks my best time,
Sunlight for my best display,
Please, hear the rustling of the leaves,
My finest hour of blossoming,
Telling you my waiting passion.
You pass by me, not noticing,
Petals fall to the earth behind you,
Strewing the ground as you depart,
Not just petals of my love, but
shards, also, of a broken heart.

Poets and their Dates

Li Bai ~ 701 to 762

Anonymous from Shi Jing ~ BC 1100 to BC 600

Qu Yuan ~ BC 340 to BC 278

Wang Bo ~ 650 to 676

He Zhizhang ~ 659 to 744

Wang Zhihuan ~ 678 to 742

Meng Haoran ~ 689 to 740

Liu Yong ~ 984 to 1053

Wang Changling ~ 698 to 757

Wang Wei ~ 701 to 761

Du Fu ~ 712 to 770

Zhang Ji ~ 766 to 830

Li Shen ~ 772 to 846

Cao Zhi ~ 192 to 232

Meng Jiao ~ 751 to 814

Su Shi ~ 1037 to 1101

Bai Juyi ~ 772 to 846

Li Yu ~ 937 to 978

Liu Yuxi ~ 772 to 842

Liu Fangping ~ Tang Dynasty

Luo Binwang ~ 626 to 687

Li Shangyin ~ 813 to 858

Li Qingzhao ~ 1084 to 1155

Zhang Jiuling ~ 673 to 740

Wei Yingwu ~ 737 to 792

Li Duan ~ 743 to 782

Song Zhiwen ~ 656 to 712

Tao Yuanming ~ 365 to 427

Yu Guangzhou ~ 1928 to 2017

Xi Murong ~ 1943 to present

About the Translators

Jade Wei Watts and Ian Watts are both qualified teachers of English to foreigners. Jade is a graduate of English and has a High School teaching certificate. She has been teaching for twenty years. Ian has an MA and a CELTA qualification. Ian teaches for Jade when he is China and not busy writing. He also teaches disadvantaged children, as a volunteer, in rural schools in the Guangxi province.

As translators, they have collaborated on their first book, published in the UK, called *Careful Drowning*, a Chinese miscellany. It contains some Song and Tang poems translated by the pair and included in this volume.

The photographs were mainly taken in Guangxi.